LOCAL EATS
LONDON

BANGERS AND MASH, PASTIES, JAFFA CAKE
AND OTHER LONDON FAVORITES

 By Natasha McGuinness
Illustrated by Danielle Kroll

yellow pear press

ISBN: 978-0-9905370-8-3

Library of Congress Cataloging-in-Publication data available upon request.

Manufactured in Hong Kong.

Design by Danielle Kroll.

This book has been set in Gill Sans and Rockwell.

10 9 8 7 6 5 4 3 2 1

Yellow Pear Press, LLC.

www.yellowpearpress.com

Distributed by Publisher's Group West

To Hayley Reese and Camryn Powell—for the many meals, conversations, significant moments, and raw experiences we shared as we ate our way through London.

TABLE OF CONTENTS

INTRODUCTION

After spending several months eating my way through the streets, markets, restaurants, and kitchens of my Londoner friends, I have some official results: contrary to the popular belief that British food is mediocre, London food is both multifaceted and delicious and those who travel there will certainly not be disappointed. I spent my time in London getting to know the ins and outs of the city and fell in love with the complex simplicity of London cuisine. I learned about the different ways in which the food of London has been influenced by other cultures around the world, and more importantly, I learned how to eat like a local. I was also given the chance to discuss the intricate dynamics of London food as a whole with a number of chefs, including head chef James Holah of Sonny's Kitchen in Barnes and the executive chef at the Ritz, John Williams.

This amazing tasting journey was filled with many memorable and diverse meals: strolling along the Thames with a gyro, clocking countless hours at tucked-away pubs and spending an afternoon like royalty at a fancy afternoon tea (details to follow.) I chose to write about food items and dishes themselves rather than specific restaurants because London is a city with a true abundance of places to dine and they are forever changing. For the sake of foodie clarity, it should be noted that this is not a comprehensive guide to London cuisine, but rather a description of traditional foods that a visitor will find to be prevalent, readily available, British, and in many cases, specific to London. This particular way of dividing up London cuisine also allows for a diner on any budget to enjoy an authentic eating experience: like a local!

MORNING FOOD

Not only does London boast myriad breakfast food options, Londoners seem to truly grasp the concept of breakfast. There is something for everyone: the health nut or the on-the-go breakfast eater, the leisurely breakfast nibbler, the picky breakfast eater and the ravenous. The list is endless. I found that some of my favorite moments and conversations in London were enjoyed over a morning meal—maybe it's the way the city feels in the morning, or the excitement of the day ahead, but either way, Londoners do it right in the morning.

FULL ENGLISH BREAKFAST

No trip to London would be complete without trying a full English breakfast at least once: be prepared to be uncomfortably stuffed and yet so satisfied. The full English breakfast is a typical Saturday-morning meal for British families, much like pancakes and bacon are to American families. A full English breakfast generally includes bacon (back bacon, which is what most Americans know as Canadian bacon), fried or poached eggs, tomatoes, mushrooms, fried bread or toast, baked beans, sausage, and is often paired with a cup of tea.

EGGS ROYALE

This morning spread is for the lover of savory over sweet breakfast foods. Eggs Royale is poached eggs served over smoked salmon, often with hollandaise sauce, all on toast. It is fresh, protein filled, and a perfect way to start off any morning!

SCRAMBLED EGGS ON TOAST

For all you picky eaters out there, scrambled eggs on toast is a great way to go! This meal can be found at most places that serve a British breakfast and is a familiar taste of home for many Americans. Although this dish is considered a typical breakfast option in London, it does not usually contain any food funny business—just a simple plate of eggs and toast! For a yummy, straight-forward, cost-effective morning meal this is certainly a good option for the less adventurous traveler.

PORRIDGE

This breakfast staple is similar to oatmeal or hot cereal. Many Londoners (and Brits as a whole) eat this simple meal as a part of their typical morning routines. It is hot, filling, and delicious. Often porridge is mixed with fruit or drizzled with honey or cream, and is a quick, easy, and affordable breakfast for those days when you are on the go for long periods of time. It is filling but does not stay with you in an uncomfortable way like many large, hearty breakfasts.

EGGS FLORENTINE ON AN ENGLISH MUFFIN

vvvvv (or really anything on an English muffin) vvvvv

You may already be a lover of English muffins, but you haven't even be-gun to experience them until you have an authentic English muffin—which is especially delicious when topped with eggs Florentine (my personal favorite), poached eggs, or fried eggs. If you are feeling a little less peckish, English muffins are always great with just melted butter and/or jam. English muffins are also a good food item to pick up at a market from an artisanal baker if you are planning to eat on the go.

CRUMPETS

These griddle cakes are similar to English muffins and are perfect for holding butter and preserves in their spongy nooks and crannies. Crumpets can be found in the cupboards of many British kitchens and are often enjoyed with a cup of tea. Plus you will sound oh-so-local when you say, "Dear, would you care to have tea and crumpets again this morning? It was such a lovely start to our day yesterday."

FRIED EGGS ON TOAST WITH MARMITE

This meal is similar to the concept of the previously listed eggs on toast but with a bit of an added twist: Londoners are known for their... umm... interesting taste in spreads, which definitely applies to Marmite, which is made of yeast extract and boasts a strong flavor that is an acquired taste. However, Marmite is worth a try because it is so popular in England. A recommendation: spread it on a small corner of your eggs on toast and give it a try before lathering it on the whole thing!

SAVORY FOOD

London is home to many dishes that are delicious, homey, hearty, and take you back to simpler times. The savory dishes in this chapter go beyond typical pub food (although you may be able to find a few of them on a pub menu), and can be found on the menus of corner restaurants, busy markets, and high-end eateries.

BANGERS AND MASH

Ahhh yes, bangers and mash—a plate piled high with steaming mashed potatoes and (generally) Cumberland sausages—a dish that you must learn if you wish to eat well while in London. This meal is very simple and straightforward and is a basic staple in many British diets but is certainly not tired or boring. Bangers and mash is generally available at any restaurant that offers British cuisine and is a must-try for visitors passing through.

SUNDAY ROAST

The perfect meal to take refuge with on a cold night. Sunday roasts are usually only available on—you guessed it—Sundays, and restaurants all over the city boast about theirs. If you had a British grandmother, this is exactly what you would expect her to cook when you went to her house for dinner. Sunday roasts usually come with the option of beef, pork, or lamb and are accompanied by vegetables (cooked peas and carrots), potatoes, Yorkshire pudding (a light, airy pastry, often served with savory British dishes), and gravy. Depending on the type of restaurant you go to, this meal ranges in quality—the reality is, a Sunday roast is worth paying a little more for if you happen to be rolling through London on a Sunday afternoon or evening.

RUMP STEAK

Basically a big juicy steak with a whole lot of fixin's. Typically a rump steak is served alongside grilled tomatoes, mushrooms, chips (known to Americans as French fries), and onion rings. All of the components of this meal go very well together and match perfectly with a pint.

HAUNCH OF VENISON

Perhaps you are not usually a big venison (a game animal, most often a deer) eater, but since Londoners make such a mean haunch of venison, intended for serious meat lovers, you should probably try it. The haunch (back leg) can be served on or off the bone and is one of the most versatile cuts of meat. This is a seasonal dish at many restaurants, which makes sense, as it is basically winter served up on a warm plate.

PORK BELLY

This is, hands down, without a doubt, the absolutey best dish in London. If you have never had pork belly before traveling here, you have been seriously missing out your entire life. Pork belly is a boneless, fatty piece of meat taken from the belly of a pig and is made up of several juicy and flavorful layers. The very top later, referred to as the "crackling," is crispy, hard, and perfect. If you don't tend to enjoy fatty pieces of meat, you'll find pork belly is the exception. While fatty, it does not have the texture that most fatty meats have. This is a must try—and then try again, and again, and again. Then, at the end of your trip, as you are boarding your flight home, you will say to yourself, "I should have eaten more of that wondrous pork belly."

HAM, EGGS, AND CHIPS

Sliced, cured ham served with fried eggs and chips (French fries). This is a no fuss, good meal that still manages to capture the essence of what it means to eat like a local.

CHICKEN, CHARDONNAY, AND PANCETTA PIE

First off, Londoners seem to have a serious obsession with pancetta. Second, this savory pie is delicious. Succulent pieces of chicken breast are cooked with a creamy chardonnay and pancetta sauce, enveloped in a piecrust, and usually served with seasonal vegetables, mashed potatoes, and a big ol' jug of gravy. This is food for the soul.

PUB FOOD

Whether you enjoy a pint or not, when in London, plan on spending some serious quality time in the pubs. If you don't, you are doing it wrong. In London, pub food is about more than just food. It is a culture, a tradition, a way of life. And there are more savory pies than you could ever imagine. Never in my life did I think that there could be so many different ways one could serve a meat pie—for the record, I don't think even those who were born, raised, and died in London have tried the copious amount of pies, pies, pies that reside on the menus of pubs all over the city. And, even if you are not a fish-loving type of person, the eating of British fish and chips in a pub is a necessary, proba-bly-going-to-throw-you-into-cardiac-arrest-from-the-amount-of-oil-you-are-consuming wonderful thing that must be tried at some point on your food journey through London.

MEAT PIES

STEAK and MUSHROOM

BEEF and STOUT PIE

CHICKEN and MUSHROOM

VENISON

Meat pies play a huge role in the London pub-food scene, and are true, classic London fare. The above four particular pies seem to be the favorites in pubs across London; each boasts a generous filling of meat, rich gravy, and a host of seasoning and flavorful vegetables, encased in a puffy, flaky crust. Meat pies are nourishing, leave your stomach warm and your heart full. These pies are worth their weight in gold.

FISH AND CHIPS

In London it is very difficult to go wrong with a heaping plate of fish and chips, which is at most pubs, as well as countless restaurants, street vendors, and take-away shops. A full traditional fish-and-chips plate comes with a side of mushy peas (this is exactly what it sounds like—mashed-up peas, which are surprisingly good), plus chip-shop extras including curry sauce, tartar sauce, pickled onions, and bread and butter.

BEEF LEG STEW

Nothing like a massive vat of beef leg stew after a long day of hunting with King Henry, am I right? Well, maybe your day wasn't quite as sporting but at least you can dine like a true carnivore with this handsome dish. Beef leg stew is hearty, wintery (for this reason it is often a seasonal dish) and sure to sustain you for the inevitable pints you are going to drink tonight. Not the plan? Well then try it for the flavorful, London-filled dish that it is!

MAC AND CHEESE

The Brits really seem to love a heaping plate of mac and cheese—and as a bonus many pubs offer this homey staple with added twists. One of the most popular of these is mac and cheese with pulled pork, topped with pork cracklings. While this may sound like a strange combination, it is surprisingly delicious and makes a fine, and fancy, pairing. Some of the other combinations to look for are cooked bacon and caramelized onions, braised leeks, chunks of lobster, peas and mint, as well as crumbles of Stilton cheese and walnut.

SMALL PLATES

Small plates are a little bit of a hidden gem in London—they are not necessarily listed clearly on menus as such, except as appetizers, but they certainly exist and are worth seeking out!

BATTERED SAUSAGES

Often dipped in an ale batter and served with different types of dipping sauces, battered sausages are generally what many Americans would consider to be mini-sized sausages. These are often paired with a pint of beer for a good, healthy, balanced diet.

BAKED HERITAGE BEET ROOT

Although every small plate in this category is lovely, heritage beet roots are the best thing ever and all but call for licking the plate and begging the chef for more! The best variation of these gems is the mixture of baked traditional British beet roots accompanied by goat curd and hazelnuts. They are simply to die for. Also, you will feel like a champ for sitting around eating fancy beet roots like the sophisticated faux-local that you are.

SMOKED SALMON AND CRAB SALAD

Avocado, sorrel, smoked salmon, and crab salad placed atop an English muffin is a light and refreshing way to cleanse your system of some of the heavier London dishes that can often take over your diet while passing through town.

VEGETABLE SOUPS

The Brits are all about offering a selection of delicious soups, which belong in the small-plate category because, though they somehow still manage to fill you up (and keep you warm), they are not large meals. Some of the more notable soups (many of these are seasonal) include pumpkin soup, portabella mushroom with garlic soup, carrot soup, and cumin soup—all of which pack a flavorful punch and embody some of the basic tastes of London.

POTTED GAME

Potting (preserving in butter) is the traditional way to ensure that fish and game keep their flavor and provides a rich, buttery finish to the final product. The best ways to eat potted game are on crackers or bread, with baked potatoes, or spread on crostini. Some of the more well known and loved of the potted games include potted pheasant, potted quail, potted rabbit, potted wild boar, potted venison, and potted trout.

SAVORY TARTS

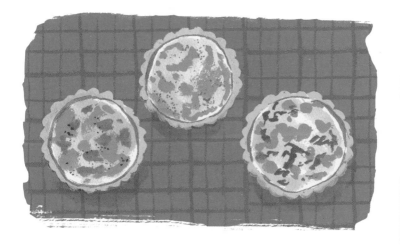

Another culinary gem of London cuisine is the savory tart. Offered in countless varieties for every taste bud, savory tarts grace the menus of the most posh of restaurants as well as the friendly neighborhood street vendor's cart, and are ideal to grab as you continue on your way. Try 'em, love 'em, swear by 'em.

PICNIC FOOD

Oh the joys of picnicking in London! The opportunities to picnic in London are as vast as the many gorgeously adorned city parks, where benches make lovely picnic spots and vantage points to watch passersby. In addition to traditional parks, the city boasts some incredible tucked-away spaces, little nooks along the Thames, and picturesque stone steps that make the perfect seat while enjoying on-the-go food like a true, in-the-know Londoner.

A favorite spot to gather picnic ingredients is Borough Market, right next to the London Bridge tube station. This massive market* is filled with artisan bakers, chefs, and culinary companies, which means that it is pretty much impossible to walk out without an arm full of mouth-watering items you didn't even know you wanted. Dangerous? Yes. Life-changingly delicious? Also yes.

* many of these stands are cash only, so come prepared!

PASTIES

These beautiful creations are meat pies meant to be eaten on the go! Pasties can be purchased at pasty shops and bakeries scattered all over London. The crust is golden and flaky and the filling is generally your choice of beef, chicken, lamb, or vegetarian, although some exotic variations can also be found. They are perfect to eat while strolling, or to pack in a basket and enjoy picnic style!

BREAD PUDDING

Bread pudding is a dessert of baked bread, soaked in caramel or other sweet rich sauce and is a great way to finish off a picnic meal. It can be found in the windows of bakeries or tucked away in markets and can always be packaged for take away. Bread pudding is not meant to be finger food as it is moist in consistency, so be sure to grab a fork and a napkin as you pack up and head out for that picturesque meal along the bank of the Thames.

FLAPJACKS

In the United States, flapjacks are thought of as an item similar to pancakes, however in London this couldn't be further from the case! Flapjacks look a lot like brownies (although they do not resemble them in taste) and are the shape of a thick granola bar. These treats come in a variety of sweet flavors, and, much like bread pudding, are a lovely dessert to toss into your picnic basket!

SAUSAGE ROLL

A sausage roll is a larger, super-fancy version of pigs-in-a-blanket—think "sows in a cashmere throw." Thick and juicy sausage, often offered in various levels of spiciness, is wrapped in flaky puff pastry and can be served hot or cold (although hot is particularly delicious). Sausage rolls are another great food to pack for a picnic or to eat while you are enjoying being immersed in the streets or parks of London.

ASSORTED BRITISH CHEESES

What screams picnic more than a basket full of little cheeses and crackers? If you'd like to include a taste of just a few of the many notable British cheeses to put in your basket, pick up wedges of Mayfield, Lord London, Sussex Blue, and Arthur's Spice Road.

DRIED, CURED CUMBERLAND BACON
AND HAM

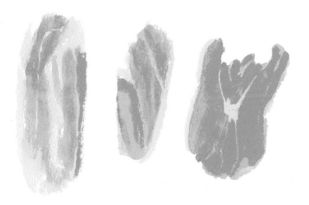

Need a morsel of fine British meat to accompany your lovely British cheeses? Dried, cured Cumberland bacon, which we, as Americans, tend to place in the category of Canadian bacon, and ham, similar to prosciutto, are the perfect additions to nibble on with your cheese and crackers. Accompany this combo with fruit or just the bottle of wine tucked into your basket!

CUMBERLAND SAUSAGE ON A STICK

This is a self-explanatory yet completely awesome food. It is a mild-but-flavorful British pork sausage on a stick—it just doesn't get any better than this. Need I say more?

PORK SCRATCHINGS

A step above traditional pork rinds, pork scratchings are crispy, salty, and found at many markets in the meat section. A great little extra to toss in your basket as you're heading out for your picnic, or, to "accidently" finish off before you have even purchased a basket.

SCOTCH EGGS

Scotch eggs are a very traditional British snack food, which London's Fortnum and Mason claims to have invented. Scotch eggs are hard-boiled eggs wrapped in a meat of your choosing, including venison, quail, wild boar, wild game, and chicken & leek. They are then covered in bread crumbs, and either baked or deep-fried.

AFTERNOON TEA

Afternoon snacks and tea-time food are, by far, the most dreamy parts of any eating experience in London. There is much history and complex culture embedded in London's afternoon tea tradition. Enjoying afternoon tea makes for a rich and unique experience, regardless of budget, and is like nothing you will have anywhere else.

Going to a nice afternoon tea is an event that occasionally merits spending a little extra cash. It requires smart-casual or semi-formal attire, and often lasts a couple hours, or more, if you opt for a venue on the posh side. That said, for a similar, but less extravagant experience, you can go to more casual tea shops throughout the city and enjoy the cultural tradition of afternoon tea quite well.

TOASTED TEA CAKES

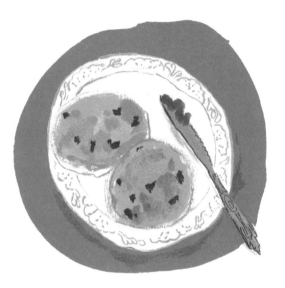

Toasted tea cakes are a great side to a pot of tea, and are unlike anything in the United States. Tea cakes have a consistency similar to an English muffin crossed with a bagel, are served with a selection of jams, and are a filling snack to tide you over until the dinner hour.

WARM SCONES

If you want to cry sweet, sweet tears of pure bliss, then warm scones are definitely for you. Generally served with clotted cream (thick cream from cow's milk that is a generally a similar consistency to room-temperature butter) and jam on the side, warm scones are a long-standing British tradition and will not disappoint.

TRADITIONAL VICTORIA SPONGE

Named after Queen Victoria, this much-loved British tea-time favorite is made of two sponge-cake layers with a filling of raspberry jam and either whipped double cream or vanilla cream in between. Delicious served alongside a cup of afternoon tea.

CARAMEL SHORTBREAD

Also known as millionaire's shortbread or caramel squares, this rich treat consists of a confectionary biscuit base with a thick layer of soft caramel and chocolate topping. Caramel shortbread is a British classic that has been a long-time favorite and should not be missed.

CINNAMON ROLLS

Although cinnamon rolls are technically native to Sweden, they are an old friend to many Londoners and are offered at countless bakeries and coffee/tea shops as a snack to go along with a warm beverage. Big, fluffy, and sweet, cinnamon rolls are a nice taste of home while still following London food trends.

LEMON DRIZZLE CAKE

One of the absolute favorites among all the (way too many) cakes in London, lemon drizzle cake is a true winner in any book. Filled with lemon curd and cream, and sometimes topped with mascarpone, lemon zest, and sugar crystals, this is the perfect balance of sweet mixed with just the right amount of lemon.

FINGER SANDWICHES

The cutest little sandwiches you ever did see (and taste!). Finger sandwiches come in different varieties (most often including cucumber, egg salad, and smoked salmon), and are often served during the afternoon hours alongside tea and a small dessert.

FULL AFTERNOON TEA VS CREAM TEA

Enjoying afternoon tea can range from a special choice on a menu, all the way to the royal treatment at the Ritz and everything in between. Full tea usually includes a three-tiered plate filled with layers of tea snacks and a variety of tea to choose from. Most places also offer an option for adding champagne, which is usually a few pounds more. Tea snacks traditionally include a selection of finger sandwiches, warm scones with clotted cream and preserves, and an assortment of freshly made cakes and pastries.

Many restaurants and cafes offer Cream Tea, which is a simpler, lighter, and less expensive version of afternoon tea. It is also more common with locals. Cream Tea includes tea, scones, clotted cream and jam.

WORLD FOOD

While many people think of typical London food as strictly of British descent, they could not be more wrong about the diverse flavors from countless cultures that help make up the taste of London. One of the things I enjoyed the most about learning to eat like a true local in London was seeing the countless varieties of food represented in markets, restaurants, and by street vendors, supplementing traditionally "British" dishes for a culinary experience unlike anywhere else in the world. These world dishes knit together London's food culture and provide a depth of flavor that is representative of the limitless diversity in London.

CHICKEN TIKKA CURRY/ MASALA

[India]

This dish is one of Britain's favorite take-out (take-away, as they say) dishes, but it also very popular in both Indian restaurants and in pubs. Chicken Tikka Curry/Masala is chunks of chicken in a curry sauce and ranges from mild to very spicy, depending on the restaurant.

PERI PERI CHICKEN

[Portugal, but it's complicated!]

The spice known as peri-peri or African bird's eye chili was discovered by the Portuguese but is made from a plant native to a number of countries in Africa, making for a complicated history. Peri-Peri chicken is usually served at a level of heat tailored to the customer's liking because it ranges from very mild to painfully spicy. Most any cut of chicken can be marinated in Peri-Peri sauce and combined with a few sides, making for nothing short of a superb meal.

THAI CHICKEN STEW

vvvvvv [Thailand] vvvvvv

Usually made with red or green curry, Thai chicken stew is rich in flavor and makes for a complete meal in a bowl! Thai chicken stew includes a wide range of spices, big chunks of chicken, and a number of vegetables.

DAMASCENE FALAFEL WRAP

vv uvv [Middle East] vv uvv

Great for vegetarians (and sometimes even vegans!), falafel started out as street food and over centuries has made its way into this exceptional wrap, found in most large London markets. While falafel is wonderful on its own, when wrapped in pita bread or flatbread and covered with vegetables and sauces, it just doesn't get any better.

GYRO

ᵛᵛᵛᵛ *[Greece]* ᵛᵛᵛᵛ

Arguably one of the most perfect meals, gyros are basically the life-blood of quick food in many European countries. They are similar to doner kebabs [Turkey], which usually have a tomato-based sauce. Shaved meat (usually chicken, lamb, or pork), yogurt sauce, seasoned chips (French fries) tucked inside, tomatoes, and onions make up this delicious on-the-go meal found all over London.

CRÊPES

✓✓✓✓✓ *[France]* ✓✓✓✓✓

Okay, it's quite possible you can put just about anything in a crêpe (a thin pancake) and it will be the best thing you ever had. Butter and sugar, Nutella and fruit, caramel, jam, or chestnut with banana or strawberry, to name a few popular sweet crêpes, as well as a variety of savory crêpes, which are often combinations of meats, vegetables, and cheeses. There is a crêpe for everyone—my favorite: Nutella and strawberry!

TURKISH DELIGHT

[Turkey]

Confections composed of sugar-dusted gummy squares, this is a long time beloved sweet in London that dates all the way back to the Ottoman Empire and even makes an appearance in C.S. Lewis's *The Chronicles of Narnia*. Turkish delight has an unusual texture that may take some getting used to. It comes in countless flavors and is a great treat to tuck away for later!

DESSERT (PUDDING)

The Brits definitely know how to wrap up a meal and you would be a fool to pass up these delicious, satisfying treats. Just a little insider tip: most places you go will call dessert "pudding." This term can be used relatively interchangeably with the word "dessert," although it seems that "dessert" has a slightly more pompous connotation. Basically, when you see "pudding" on a menu, it is not referring to the delightfully creamy concoction your mom used to pack in a plastic snack cup in your lunch; it means "Look over here you sugar-craving buffoon and order every single item on this list."

BONOFFEE PIE

This dessert pie somehow manages to be simultaneously rich and light, and is sometimes served with a scoop of vanilla ice cream. Bonoffee pie is made of bananas, cream, and dulce de leche (toffee made from boiled sweetened condensed milk) in a crust of pastry or crumbled cookies.

ETON MESS

One of the unparalleled desserts in London, Eton Mess certainly will not disappoint. This heavenly combination is a mixture of strawberries, crushed pieces of meringue, and cream in one big, happy mess of perfection.

BRAMLEY APPLE PIE
OR CRUMBLE

Much like good ol' American apple pie or crumble, but with lovely, tart Bramley apples (which originated in Nottinghamshire). Bramley pie is often topped with a dollop of heavy whipped cream.

STICKY TOFFEE PUDDING

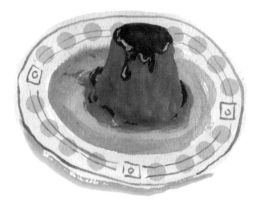

One word: "YES." Eat this. Sticky toffee pudding is a steamed dessert made of moist sponge cake and finely chopped dates, drowned in toffee sauce. This masterpiece is also accompanied by either vanilla custard or vanilla ice cream, which is important because this heavy pudding is too sweet without the balance of the cool, lighter custard or ice cream.

JAFFA CAKE

These small, cookie-sized cakes are covered with a layer of dark chocolate and orange jelly and are a great dessert to eat when you want a sweet little bite at the end of your meal or tea time!

LEMON TART

A true classic that just can't be outdone—Londoners take pride in their superiority with this tart and are dedicated to making the best version around. The lemon is tangy, sweet, and buttery, the crust flaky. In short: eat this.

SALTED CARAMEL TART

The creamy, almost toffee-like center of this tart is complemented by flecks of sea salt and a flaky, buttery crust—this dessert falls nothing short of a heavenly dream. I want to experience the mouth-watering goodness all over again just writing about it.

SPOTTED DICK

If you can get past the suggestive name of this dessert, you will be in for a real treat. A lovely British classic, spotted dick is a steamed fruit sponge usually made with raisins or currants, and is often served with custard.

MIDNIGHT SNACKS

Whether it is popping by the corner pub just before it closes, or whipping up a little something in the kitchen to tide you over until breakfast, midnight snacks are a true pleasure and a delightful way to add an extra few hundred calories to your day—after all, you deserve it; you probably walked the equivalent of at least seven marathons trying to switch tube lines throughout the day.

BEANS ON TOAST

Beans on toast seems to be a bit of an obsession among the Brits, and is a nice way to end a day of sightseeing—if you are a freak of nature and enjoy a can of syrupy baked beans dumped on a piece of buttered toast.

GRILLED MUSHROOMS
WITH BAKED GOAT CHEESE

Although this gem is a little harder to find on typical pub menus, it is a delectable end to any day spent in London and is worth looking around for.

PORK CHEEKS

Often slow cooked and even served on small pieces of toast, pork cheeks seem to be a trend among the adventurous-eater crowd. Although you may be skeptical at first, this classy last-call plate might quickly became one of your favorite ways to wrap up chilly London days.

POTATO WEDGES

Potato wedges are potato wedges are potato wedges—true—but it's a nice way to catch a more familiar taste while still rocking that London vibe you have been expertly cultivating. They're often sprinkled with parsley, cumin or sea salt and wrapped in paper for munching on the go.

HOG ROAST SANDWICH

The only way to conclude this book is with a description of the absolute true pleasure of ending the day with a hog roast sandwich, which you will swear was made by divine hands. Think pulled-pork sandwich somehow made infinitely better with bits of cracklin'. Many vendors have their own special version of this delicious creation, so even if you are a picky eater, go all out on this sandwich and order it with whatever toppings they recommend—after all, by now you are practically a local!

ACKNOWLEDGEMENTS

Many thanks and serious kudos to the following people—without whom the entirety of this book would be one big, fat, pipe dream: Danielle Kroll, the best person to bring everything I hoped this book could be to life; Kim Carpenter, who read, read again, and re-read the many phases of my manuscript; my home girl Lisa McGuinness for being the most badass and loving mom there ever was; and to my dad, Matt McGuinness, the world's best man and the only reason my odd sense of humor has lasted as long as it has. Thank you as well to the many chefs who took the time to talk me through their menus and answer my endless lists of questions. To my flat mates and dear friends in London, who put up with a foreigner in their kitchen, and helped me to see what it means to eat in an authentic, British way. Maybe most importantly, however, a true and deep thank you to Hayley Reese and Camryn Powell, who willingly spent months by my side eating, discussing, discovering, and often painstakingly recording our love of London foods. Finally, a sincere thank you to Sydney Boral, Morgan Kertel, and Cheryl Duncan, who will never know the incredible depths that their individual and collective support and love have had in my life.

INDEX